A Dog's Book of Wisdom

VOLUME I

*Life Advice from
Margaret the Pug*

A Dog's Book of Wisdom: Life Advice from Margaret the Pug

©2024 Tom Noser

Published by Clovercroft Publishing, Franklin, Tennessee

Printed in the United States of America

978-1-956370-15-7 (print)

To all the people who drop food on the floor when they eat. Thank you. — Margaret the Pug

DOGS DON'T WRITE
MANY BOOKS. WE
ENJOY LIFE AND LEARN
ALL WE NEED BY
LIVING. MAMMAS DON'T
GET EVERYTHING LIVING, SO
THEY LOOK IN BOOKS

A Note on the Translation

Translating from Dog to English is incredibly difficult, even when you're translating for a dog you've lived with for eighteen years. Dogs communicate with gestures, and one gesture can mean many things. Dogs don't use adjectives or adverbs; their language is very colorful. Dogs have no concept of lying but will change the facts to fit their purposes. Although for clarity I use "I" when Margaret refers to herself, "we" is closer to her true meaning; she makes little distinction between herself and the things around her. This is only a partial list of the challenges facing a dog translator. If something in this book doesn't make sense, blame the English language. Everything made sense when I heard it from Margaret.

Tom Noser
Nashville, TN
2023

Preface

Ever since I was a kid, I've wanted to know what dogs think. Now I know. My seventeen year old Pug Margaret thinks like the philosopher Michel de Montaigne because she's Montaigne reincarnated.

One spring afternoon while reading on my porch, Margaret came in to sit with me as she often did when I was thinking or working. I heard a voice in my head I had not heard before. I looked up from the page and realized Margaret was speaking to me. Her lips didn't move, but her voice was clear, skeptical, and humorous. I should have been terrified that I was losing my mind, but because it was Margaret and she was speaking in a voice I loved— Montaigne's voice— I was delighted. Her humor, curiosity, good company, and disdain for "the common herd," were pure Montaigne. She made me aware of my ridiculousness and helped me laugh at it. She had to be him.

We're all prone to assign unusual significance to the ones we love. It's common to hear a father or mother, brother or sister eulogized as a remarkable hero when to a stranger the dead person's life seems entirely ordinary. Love transforms how we see things. I loved Margaret, and her life was an inspiration to me. Where I was sometimes lonely, she was comfortable being alone. Where I was afraid to speak my mind, she said just what she meant. Where I was ashamed of my weaknesses, she never aspired to perfection. Where I avoided conflict, she was brave. When our kids were small we took Margaret to a boarding house for dogs so our family could go on vacation. Margaret sought out the largest animal in the group, a German Shepard, and barked at it until the dog cowered under a couch. Once she established her dominance, Margaret was tolerant of other dogs, except for one Poodle who lived a few houses away from us. Margaret and this Poodle had an unexplainable and continuous feud that surfaced as spasms of barking, lunging, and teeth bearing whenever they saw each other. Eventually I decided that my dog was a "breedist," a kind of canine racist, and had an unmotivated and irrational hatred of Poodles just because they're Poodles. Somehow, because she shared this stubborn human vice, I loved her even more.

Margaret had many more virtues than vices. From the age of four months well into her seventeenth year she made only one mess in the house that I can remember. She was easy to train for the things she wanted to learn. She was excellent company on walks and took her leash well after she had time to sniff. If she got outside the backyard fence she would walk around to the front of the house and scratch on the door to be let back in. Like Montaigne she valued friendship, conversation, and time to think above all else. Most importantly, she made me a better and wiser person by making me happy. I hope she makes you happier and wiser, too.

Tom Noser

CHAPTER ONE

"WHAT WOULD A DOG DO?"

"If you want to be good, do what a dog would do.
If you want to be right, I can't help you."
- Margaret the Pug

Dogs don't write many books. We enjoy life and learn all we need by living. Humans don't get everything they need from living, so they look in books for what's missing. They don't find it because there are not enough books written by dogs.

This book is about the mind of a dog; it follows no particular order. Our minds roam and follow our desires, which is the way of wisdom. Humans are very unwise. Humans have no instinct and bad training. My hope is that humans can be trained to think like dogs, which is the right way to think, and if they obey, humans will be as content as dogs. We dogs will be happier, too.

You can learn a lot from dogs. Here is an example: All creatures feel pain. Pain can be either good or bad. Being hungry is a good pain because it tells me to do something: eat. Being bitten by another dog is a bad pain because I can't do anything about the pain.

Even with food, health, entertainment, shelter, companionship, and no dog bites, humans feel pain, pain they think is bad, but may be good. Humans spend too much time with pain, which means we dogs spend too much time with humans who are in pain.

Humans worry and fret. Humans are anxious. Some dogs are nervous, but only because they have not learned endurance. I am a Pug, and Pugs know endurance, so I know endurance. Plus, I'm very old, and you must learn endurance to be very old.

"Pain is a great teacher even though it hurts."

- Muhammad Ali's Alaskan Malamute

I use quotes to say things I could say myself, but I want them to sound better, so I say the words came from someone famous. All my quotes are from other dogs, so you will never know if they are right.

My favorite phrase is "good Pug." I can't hear it enough. I like "good Pug" better than "good dog" because good Pug is about Pugs. "Good dog" is fine, but "good Pug" is better. I want Tom—the man I live with—to learn what good means. Good means "being like a dog," and very good means "being like a Pug." When Tom acts like a Pug, he will earn praise like "good Tom" and maybe get a treat he can share with me.

A good dog doesn't complain. A good dog is tidy and only makes messes where it should. A good dog takes a leash easily and does not disappear when it's off a leash. A good dog disciplines when necessary, helps when it should, and never helps or disciplines too much. A good dog does what it must and what it enjoys and nothing else.

I will show you how to be good. Ask yourself three questions: Is someone in my pack in danger? Am I in danger? What do I feel like doing? If someone in the pack is in danger, remove the danger. If no one in the pack is in danger go to the second question. If you are danger, remove yourself from danger. If you are not in danger, do whatever you like. Do what you must, then do what you like, and don't do anything else.

People don't know how to be good unless dogs tell them what to do. People are very busy. Dogs are never busy. Being busy is doing things without knowing what you are doing. People stay busy because they cannot be still. Some good things come from being busy, but not very much. I am glad to keep Tom company while he's busy because keeping him company is more important than anything Tom does while he's busy.

You won't understand this next thing because it is very Dog, but I will tell you anyway. There is no you—there is only we. You don't exist by yourself. You are yourself and everything else at the same time. So there's no reason to be lonely or feel sorry for yourself. Tom spends a lot of time sitting like I do, but he often feels sorry for himself, and I never do that. Tom will have to read this whole book to know how to be good.

Being good will make him happy, and even if it does not make him happy, being good and unhappy is better than being bad and unhappy.

"When I feel good because I was bad, I feel good only a little while, and I have to be bad again to feel good again. When I'm good, I feel good for a long time, and I don't have to do anything else."

- Plato's Pomeranian

I will tell you a story to show how it's hard to be bad and happy for long, just like it's hard to be unhappy for long when you are good.

The Poodle Who Liked to Bite People

A Poodle who likes to bite people goes out for a walk with their human. No one knows why the Poodle likes to bite people; it's a Poodle, and there is no point in thinking about why Poodles do what they do. The person who lives with the Poodle does not know the Poodle well, so he is surprised when the Poodle bites a woman on the leg. The woman says to the man, "Your dog bit me! You should kill it."

"My Poodle and I are in love," says the man. "I will feel bad if I kill him. I will put a bell on him instead so people will know he's the Poodle who bites. Then people can stay away from him."

The woman agrees that putting a bell on the Poodle is better than killing him, even if the Poodle is a Poodle and not a real dog, and the man who loves the Poodle is very foolish to be in love with a Poodle. The next day, the Poodle goes to the park with its bell on. The Poodle is very happy to have the bell and shows off its bell to all the other dogs. "Look at my beautiful bell," says the Poodle to an old Pug. "Don't you wish you had a bell like this?"

"How did you get the bell?" the old Pug asks. Since this Pug is so wise and beautiful, we'll call her Margaret.

"I bit a woman on the leg, and my human gave me this bell as a prize," says the Poodle.

"That bell is not a prize," says Margaret the Pug. "It's a warning to others that you bite. That's why no one wants to pet you."

The Poodle thinks for a moment, which is very difficult for a Poodle to do, but he does it anyway because Margaret is such a good teacher. It's true that no one will come near the Poodle now that he has a bell.

"I felt good about my bell before you told me what it is," says the Poodle to Margaret. "Now I feel bad, and it's your fault."

"It's not my fault you feel bad," says Margaret. "It's your fault for biting the woman, so your human had to put that bell on you."

"No, it's your fault I feel bad, no matter what you say," says the Poodle. With that, the Poodle turns around and walks away in a swishy manner that tells Margaret he thinks he's better than her. Margaret feels bad for a moment because no one likes to be walked away from in a swishy manner. Then Margaret feels good again because she knows she never bites anyone for fun, and she knows the Poodle will always be bad, so it can never be happy for long.

What does this story mean? It means some dogs don't know when to get excited—at the chance to be good or the chance to bite a woman's leg. And it means that a dog who knows what is good will never be sad for long, even when a Poodle walks away from her in a swishy manner.

CHAPTER TWO

NOTHING IS QUITE A LOT

"Don't believe anything a dog says. Just watch and be still."
- Margaret the Pug

Most things humans say and do don't need to be done or said.

"Can you believe all the time we waste being busy?"

- John D. Rockefeller's Rottweiler

Humans can open peanut butter jars. That is a very good skill to have. Humans drive cars. That's a good skill, too, when they take me with them, and a bad skill when they leave me at home. Humans cannot sleep comfortably on the floor, while I can, and sleeping on the floor is a good skill when you are in a room with no bed or when it's too much bother to get in bed. What's worth doing depends on what I want; the less I want, the less I have to do.

Humans think they are saying something when they talk, but really they're just making noise. Dogs don't talk and say a lot. I am comfortable with silence because I come from nothing. I can stare at something and see the nothing inside it. Humans cannot see nothing because they don't like nothing. Humans always want something to be there, so they fill up empty spaces with things like their voices or a couch.

> *"The best thing to fill an empty space is fried chicken. The next best thing is nothing."*
>
> - *Benjamin Franklin's Beagle*

Nothing is the space between things. Everything is mostly nothing. Nothing holds us up. I will tell you a story to show what I mean.

Two Pelicans and a Pug

Two pelicans live near a lake that's drying up. With them is a Pug puppy who is separated from her family. The Pug puppy is young, pretty, and lovable, so we will call her Margaret. The pelicans want to fly to the beach because there is an ocean full of fish there, and the dry lake has few fish and no food for Margaret.

"Let us take the cute Pug puppy with us to the beach," says one pelican to the other. I will call him Pete. "Then we can have fish and the company of a cute Pug puppy," says Pelican Pete.

"What will the Pug puppy eat?" asks the other pelican who I will call Floyd.

"There is always plenty of food at the beach, like French fries and ice cream," says Pelican Pete. Pelican Floyd agrees and nods his head as he has been to the beach many times and has never seen a hungry dog there. The two pelicans then go to Margaret to tell her their idea.

"You are cute, and we want to take you to the beach," says Pelican Pete.

"And if you stay at this dry lake, you will have nothing to eat or drink," adds Pelican Floyd.

"I want to find my family," says Margaret.

"They are probably at the beach," says Pelican Floyd. "There are always people at the beach." Pelican Pete nods, and Margaret nods, too, even though she has never been to the beach.

"How will we get to the beach?" asks Margaret.

"Floyd and I will hold a stick in our beaks," says Pelican Pete. "You can hold the stick in your mouth. We will carry you to the beach as long as you don't open your mouth to talk. If you open your mouth, you will fall."

Margaret thinks this is an excellent idea. The two birds find a stick that fits well in their beaks and is strong enough to support Margaret while the pelicans fly. Once they find the stick, Pelican Floyd tells Margaret, "Hold the stick tight and don't say anything!" Margaret already has the stick in her mouth and nods her head. Then the two pelicans pick up the stick, one pelican on one end of the stick and the other pelican on the other end. The two pelicans flap their wings and take off, holding it in their beaks while Margaret bites down on the stick. The three animals rise into the air, and the pelicans begin flying to the beach.

The wind tickles Margaret all up and down her stomach. Soon, Margaret has to pee. She looks at Floyd and Pete and tries to get their attention, but neither bird looks at her because they are busy flying. So Margaret opens her mouth to tell the pelicans she needs to pee, but instead of saying, "I need to pee," she says, "Yipe! Yipe! Yipe!" because now she is falling.

Pete and Floyd dive through the air, chasing after Margaret. Pete opens his mouth wide and catches her in his bill. Then all three animals drift down to the ground, the two pelicans and Margaret in Pete's mouth.

When he lands, Pelican Pete opens his mouth, and Margaret rolls out on the ground.

"Are you all right, Margaret?" asks Pelican Pete.

"Just a moment," answers Margaret, who disappears behind a rock. When she finishes her business, she comes back out and tells the two pelicans she's fine. "I opened my mouth to tell you I needed to pee," she says.

"It's too windy up there to hear you," says Pelican Pete. "Next time you need to pee, pull on the stick, and we will look at you. We can tell if you need to pee or not." Little Margaret agrees because she knows important things like telling someone you need to pee can be communicated with a look and don't need words.

The two pelicans pick up the stick and ask little Margaret, "Are you ready to go again?"

"How do you stay in the air?" asks Margaret. "I don't see anything to hold you up."

"We push against nothing with our wings," says Pelican Floyd.

"Nothing holds us up," adds Pelican Pete. Pelican Pete can see that his answer scares little Margaret. "Don't worry," he says. "There is a lot of nothing, so there is a lot to hold us up."

Margaret thinks nothing must be the something she felt tickling her stomach that made her need to pee. If nothing can make her pee, then nothing can hold the pelicans in the air, too. Margaret bites down on the stick, the pelicans flap their wings, and the three of them go into the air again.

Margaret enjoys riding through the sky, feeling the nothing all around her.

There is nothing above her and nothing below her. Nothing blows on her stomach, and nothing makes her ears flap. Eventually, Margaret's mouth gets dry, and her jaws get tired of holding herself up. Margaret thinks about nothing and sees nothing all around her. Then she doesn't notice her dry mouth, and her jaw doesn't hurt so much.

Margaret's eyes get dry from the sunlight and the wind. So she closes her eyes and sees the nothing behind her eyes. Her nothing makes her forget that her eyes are dry. Then Margaret opens her eyes and sees a family of people on the land below. She wonders if they are her family, so she opens her mouth to ask, but instead of asking, she says, "Yipe! Yipe! Yipe!" because she is falling again.

Pete and Floyd swoop down again. Floyd catches Margaret in his mouth. The three animals land, Floyd opens his mouth, and Margaret rolls out.

"Why did you open your mouth again?" asks Pelican Pete.

"I saw a family and wanted to ask if they were my family," says little Margaret. Pelican Pete and Pelican Floyd agree that this is a very good reason to open your mouth, but not when you're being carried through nothing by two birds going to the beach.

"That family must be going to the beach, too," says Pelican Pete. "You can see if they are your family when we get there."

Again the three animals pick up the stick and confirm they are all ready to fly to the beach without having to say anything since they know each other well and can say what's important without words. Into the air they go, riding on nothing, and a short while later, Margaret smells the ocean and hears the waves. They have arrived at the beach. The three animals land and drop the stick. Margaret wants to thank the pelicans for carrying her all the way to the beach, but she does not have to because the pelicans felt how happy and excited she was when they circled the beach before they landed. After dropping Margaret on the beach, the pelicans take off and fly toward the waves to look for fish. Little Margaret is not angry because she knows they must be hungry, just as she is hungry after the long flight.

Then Margaret looks down the beach and sees a family sitting on chairs under an umbrella. It's the family she saw while flying to the beach. She trots towards them, thinking, "How will I be able to ask the people if they are my family? I don't speak People." But she won't have to ask because words are not needed to communicate what's important.

A boy sitting with the family sees Margaret running along the beach. He takes a handful of French fries and goes to her. He knows Margaret is hungry. Margaret and the boy reach each other and stop. They look each other in the eyes and smile. Margaret cocks her head, and the boy gives her a French fry. Margaret smacks her lips and gobbles the French fry down. The two are now in love. They go back together to the boy's family, and without having to say anything, Margaret is welcomed into the boy's pack because animals who understand each other don't need to say anything. Nothing is enough.

What does this story mean? It means when you're with people you love, you don't have to say much. And it means when two pelicans carry you by a stick, keep your mouth shut or you'll fall.

CHAPTER THREE

FORGETFULNESS

"If you remember what's important, you'll never forget what's important."
- Margaret the Pug

I don't remember details, but I remember what's important. I never forget breakfast or dinner. I never forget to sleep. I don't forget to come into the room with the couch when Tom watches his screen. Tom forgets things all the time. Often Tom says, "Treat time!" and opens the door to the room with the smelly clothes, which is where I'm sent when I've made Tom mad. Many times, when I go into the room with the smelly clothes, Tom closes the door after me and leaves me alone with no treat. Tom is not very bright. He can't remember anything for a moment.

> *"Did I forget something? Oh, wait…*
> *what did I just say?"*
>
> *- Every Human Ever*

Humans say, "Treat time! Treat time!" and then lock their dogs in the room with the smelly clothes. Humans are the only animals I know who say, "Treat time!" and then forget to give a treat. Cats never give treats—they're awful—but they don't forget like humans. I love humans better than cats even though humans forget, but I love eye drops better than cats. I will tell you a story to show how humans like Tom always forget things, but dogs never forget.

Peace in the Land

A chicken is sitting on the branch of a tree when a woman approaches it, holding a butcher knife. The woman and the chicken are being watched by a dog lying in the shade nearby.

"Come down from that tree, little chicken. It's time for us to eat," says the woman. The chicken does not move, which makes sense since chickens don't understand what people say.

"Peace has been declared in all the land, and no one will eat anyone anymore," says the woman to the chicken. The dog has not heard that peace has been declared in the land. The woman must have forgotten to tell him. It's strange the woman would tell the chicken about peace before telling her dog, but people are always forgetting to tell their dogs things, so it's not that strange. "Come down from that tree, little chicken. Join us at the feast to celebrate!"

The dog cannot tell if the chicken understands the woman, but it probably does not because the chicken stays in the tree. Then there's a loud noise and much shouting from the edge of the yard. A man runs toward the woman, the dog, and the chicken in the tree. "A bear is coming!" yells the man. The woman and the man and the dog run in the house together and shut the door. While the man and the woman peep out the windows into the yard, the dog curls up to think. "Someone must have forgotten to tell the bear that peace has been declared and no one will harm anyone anymore," thinks the dog. "Or maybe the bear came for the feast, and there's not enough for him as well as us."

After some time, the man goes outside again and comes back a few minutes later with a dead chicken. Soon dinner is ready, and the man and the woman sit at the table, and the dog lies under the table, all ready to eat roast chicken. It's not a very big chicken; it's like the chicken in the tree, who was also not very big. It must be that there was not enough food for the bear as well as the dog and his humans, so that's why everyone ran inside. After the man and the woman finish their chicken, the man puts his plate on the floor, and the dog licks up the last shreds of chicken. As he's enjoying the scents and flavors of the chicken shreds, the dog thinks, "This is delicious chicken. It's made us very happy. And that has brought peace to the land."

What does this story mean? Many times people say one thing and then do something else, like say no one will hurt anyone anymore, and then they eat roast chicken. Sometimes they do this because they forgot what they said, and sometimes they do it because the chicken is too delicious not to eat.

Here is what Tom says about this story.

"The farmer's wife did not forget about peace being declared in the world. She lied to the chicken so she could get it to come out of the tree."

"What is a lie?" I say.

"A lie is something that's not true," Tom says.

"What's not true?" I ask.

"Lots of things. People say things that aren't true all the time, like 'That was delicious,' when it was really just average."

"I'm confused," I say. "Food is always delicious."

"OK, that was a bad example," Tom says. "Suppose I say, 'Oh, I don't mind that you messed in the house,' when really it bothers me."

"Are you thinking about me messing in the house?" I ask.

"No, I'm not. You don't mess in the house much, and when you do, it's usually my fault," Tom says.

"Then you don't mind that I mess in the house," I say.

"Well, that's true."

"So, what is not true?" I ask.

"I didn't think it would be this hard to explain," says Tom. "Here's something. The sky is purple—that's a lie. Or saying it's raining now when it's actually sunny. Those are lies."

"The sky is purple in some places," I say. "I see purple even if you don't. And I can see it's not raining, so saying, 'It's raining,' is not a lie. It's dumb."

"You really have no idea what a lie is," Tom says.

"No, I don't," I say. "And that's the truth."

CHAPTER FOUR

ONLY CARRY WHAT YOU NEED

"Why do you carry all those things that don't do you any good?
Look at me. I don't even have pockets."
- Margaret the Pug

I like people. I like Tom particularly. Tom is sad sometimes. I used to be sad when Tom was sad. Then I learned if I was sad when Tom was sad, we were both sad, and that wasn't good. Being sad can be good when it teaches me something. Sadness tells me what's valuable, what things to keep and what to give away. I will tell you a story and show you what I mean.

Two Dogs, Two Backpacks, and the Weight of the World

Two dogs are carrying packs while walking along a path in the woods. One dog tells the other dog, "This pack is making me sad. It weighs a lot, and I don't know what's in it."

The other dog responds, "That's too bad. I feel sad knowing that you feel sad."

"Can you take this pack off my back?" asks the first dog.

"I can't," says the second dog. "I don't have hands to unbuckle the straps."

Now both dogs feel sad because neither has hands to unbuckle the packs from their backs. The dogs tramp on a little bit farther until the first dog lies down and stops.

"I can't go any more," he says. "

Why not?" asks the second dog, who's not quite so sad because she likes walking in the woods and carrying a pack.

"I'm just too tired," answers the first dog.

"Our packs are about the same size," says the second dog. "Why should you be more tired than me?"

"My pack has more in it," says the first dog. "That's why I'm more tired."

The second dog says,"Let's tear open each other's packs. Then we can see if one really has more than the other one."

The first dog agrees that this is a good idea, so the two dogs go to work gnawing on each other's packs.

Each dog chews and gnaws and pulls and tugs, working to tear holes and pull out whatever is in the packs. Around the same time, each dog finishes making a hole in the other dog's pack, pulls something from it, and drops it on the ground. This makes the holes in the packs even bigger. After each dog pulls a few things out of the other's pack, both dogs shake themselves and get everything in their packs to fall out on the ground. Then the ground is covered in things that fell out of their packs. The dogs stand back from the mess and survey the scattered items together.

"I can't tell what came out of my pack," says the second dog.

"Neither can I," says the first. "But I don't feel sad anymore. I feel great."

"I do too," says the second dog.

"Yes, it's much easier with nothing in our packs," says the first dog. "What should we do now?"

"Let's look through what came out of our packs and see if there's anything we want to keep. Then we can pick that up and carry it home in our mouths," says the second dog.

"That's an excellent idea," says the first dog. The two dogs then begin sniffing through the things that came out of their packs, and each finds a bag of dog treats they want to keep. But instead of carrying the treats home, they tear the bags open and eat all the treats inside.

"I'm not sad anymore, but I'm very full," says the first dog.

"I was not sad to begin with, but I'm very full now, too," says the second dog. "Let's run home and run off this full

feeling." Both dogs quickly trot home, happy together with no packs on their backs.

What does this story mean? Don't let anyone put something on your back that you don't want to carry, and if you do end up with something you can't get rid of, ask a friend to tear open your pack so you can shake it out.

"There's more than one way to lick an ice cream bowl,
but I like my way best."
- Margaret the Pug

CHAPTER FIVE

By Different Paths We Arrive at the Same Place

Two dogs from the same litter live with a man who works outside. Every day the man gets up and goes into his fields to move things around. One of his dogs has lots of energy. He loves to get up with the man and go with him while he moves things around. The other dog is lazy and likes to stay in bed. When the man comes downstairs at the start of the day, the dog with lots of energy is already awake. He greets the man with a smile and wags his tail, excited about the day. After breakfast, the man and the dog go outside, get into something with a motor, and ride around the fields.

Sometime later, the dog who likes to sleep gets up, eats breakfast, and goes to the front door. He waits for the man to come home for lunch. When the man comes home, he comes inside and eats lunch at the table with the lazy dog while the energetic dog waits outside. The lazy dog lays at the farmer's feet, looking at him and loving him while he eats.

After the man finishes eating, he puts his plate on the floor and rubs the lazy dog on the head. Then he goes back outside and gets into something else with a motor with the energetic dog. They leave and don't come back until the stars come out. While they are gone, the lazy dog usually lays on the front porch or in the grass. He looks across the fields, at the animals in their pens, or at nothing much in particular. Sometimes the children who live with the man come out and talk to the lazy dog, and sometimes the cats who live in the barn pester the lazy dog, but most days, very little happens, and the lazy dog is content.

When the man and the energetic dog come home, they go inside together, and the lazy dog follows behind them. The man refreshes their water bowl, fills their food bowls with kibble, and goes into the kitchen. When the energetic dog finishes his meal, he tells his brother, "It must be dull staying here at the house. You should come with us tomorrow when we ride around the fields."

"No, thank you," says the lazy dog. "I like doing nothing."

"Ugh," answers his brother. "I couldn't stand it."

"We are from the same litter. Yet you are restless and full of energy," says the dog who likes to sleep.

"And you are slow and content to do nothing," answers the dog who likes to get up.

"We both get the food and love we need," answers the dog who sleeps. "We just get them in different ways."

"We certainly do," says his brother.

What does this story mean? You and I can want the same thing, and we can both get it by following different paths. Both dogs want the love and companionship of the farmer. One dog gets up and rides all day with the farmer. The other dog sleeps in and watches the farmer eat lunch. One dog is lazy, and the other has lots of energy, so they seem different, but the dogs want the same things, and they are good company. They both love the farmer, and they both love the farm. One dog is not better than the other because he has energy. The dogs are equal, and by different paths, they arrive at the same place.

CHAPTER SIX

How I Love My Friends Even When They're Wrong

"We can all be wrong sometimes, and most of us are wrong
most of the time, which is why I love everyone all the time.
And so I'm never wrong."
- Margaret the Pug

Friendship is the best, most important, and most enjoyable thing there is. There is nothing I would rather do than be with a friend.

Companions can be replaced, and I don't notice the difference. Friends can't be replaced because I notice when they are gone. I can't replace myself with another animal and not notice that I am gone, so I know I am a friend to myself. Tom is my friend because I would miss Tom if he was replaced with another animal.

*"You can have only one favorite of anything.
Choose wisely."*

- Napoleon Bonaparte's Bichon Frisé

I have one friend in every pack; the other dogs are companions. Tom is my friend in my human pack; the other humans are companions. Tom does many dumb things, but I don't want him to change. If Tom was like me, he would be happier, but he would be less interesting.

Here is a story to show what friends are. This is a story about dogs, but it works for people, too. It's also a story to show why I don't care if my friends are dumb, and you shouldn't either.

Four Dogs and a Barn

A pack of dogs has lost its leader. It's time to decide who the new leader is. One of the dogs, a long-haired Dachshund, is friends with a big, dumb Newfoundland. The Dachshund loves the Newfoundland and does not care that he is dumb. Being dumb is part of who the Newfoundland is, so the Dachshund loves the Newfoundland's dumbness and does not think it's a problem. The little Dachshund wants to make the Newfoundland happy, so he tells the pack that the Newfoundland should be the leader since he is the biggest and strongest of the dogs. All the other dogs know the Newfoundland is the dumbest dog, but the other dogs don't care much about who leads them. They agree with the Dachshund, and the Newfoundland becomes their leader. All the dogs are happy with the choice except for a young Pug. This Pug is wise and brave, so we will call her Margaret. Margaret wants to be the leader, too, but no one will vote for her because she makes a lot of noise when she breathes. Margaret has a friend who is a mutt with the legs of a corgi and the body of a Labrador who the dogs call Helmut. After the Newfoundland is made leader, Helmut and Margaret huddle together to talk.

"Would you vote for me to be leader?" Margaret asks Helmut.

"Of course," says Helmut. "You are my friend."

"What about the Newfoundland?"

"I voted for him because everyone else was voting for him, and he's so simple. I like to see him happy," says Helmut.

"I should be the leader," says Margaret. "I'm smarter than the Newfoundland and more brave. It takes ten of me to make one of him, but I fight just as hard." Margaret has never been in a fight, but dogs only say things that are true, so it must be true.

"Let's give the Newfoundland a chance to be leader," suggests Helmut, and Margaret agrees because Pugs who want to be leaders will give another dog a chance, even if that dog is big and dumb.

Helmut and Margaret go to the Newfoundland and tell him they are happy he is the leader. The Newfoundland has already forgotten he's the new leader, so he doesn't respond. Margaret wants to help the Newfoundland be a good leader, so she tells the Newfoundland about a barn nearby with good things to eat like bugs, dead animals, and garbage. The Newfoundland is very excited to hear about the barn and tells Margaret to take him there right away. He does not tell any of the other dogs where he's going or invite them to come along because he's dumb. Helmut follows Margaret and the Newfoundland because Helmut is a good friend and wants to help Margaret.

Soon Margaret, the Newfoundland, and Helmut arrive at the barn. Helmut and Margaret take the Newfoundland to a hole in the side of the barn that's big enough for short-legged dogs to squeeze through. The Newfoundland looks at the hole and then looks at the two other dogs.

"What's that?" asks the Newfoundland.

"That's how we get into the barn," says Margaret. "I'll show you," but before she can get to the hole, the Newfoundland, who's remembered that he's the leader and wants to make a good show, forces himself in between Margaret and the opening, pushes with all his strength, and gets himself wedged in the hole.

"Hurmfff. Hurmff, hurmff," grunts the Newfoundland. "I'm stuck."

"Of course you're stuck," says Margaret. "You're too big!"

Just then, the other dogs come trotting up, led by the Dachshund who is friends with the Newfoundland.

"Fathead," which is the Newfoundland's name, "how did you get stuck there?" asks the Dachshund.

"The Pug pushed me," says Fathead the Newfoundland. It's hard to understand Fathead because his front half is inside the barn, and his back end is outside, but all the dogs can tell is that Fathead is upset.

The Dachshund turns and confronts Margaret. "How could you do this? Fathead is our leader. You are a bad dog!"
"She's not a bad dog," says Helmut, defending his friend.
"Yes, she is," says the Dachshund. "Besides, you are her friend, so you would say anything."

"I am her friend, and I would say anything to help her, just as you are Fathead's friend, and you would say anything to help him," says Helmut. "But I'm also a dog, and dogs always tell the truth."

All the dogs nod their heads and agree that dogs always tell the truth.

"So what do we do now?" asks the Dachshund. Fathead also wants to know, as he is tired of being stuck.

"Fathead the Newfoundland cannot be our leader because he is too dumb," says Margaret. The dogs nod their heads in agreement, even the Dachshund and Fathead, who is nodding his head inside the barn.

"Who should be our leader?" asks a dog from the pack.

"Margaret should be our leader," says Helmut. "She's clever, even if she is a loud breather."

All the dogs agree with this, and Margaret is made the new leader.

"How will we save Fathead?" asks the Dachshund.

"Yes, how will you save me?" asks Fathead from inside the barn. The dogs snicker when Fathead asks this because even though no dog wants to crawl into a hole and get stuck, it's funny to see it when it happens to another dog—particularly a dog as big and dumb as Fathead.

"I have a human friend nearby, and she will do something," says Margaret. The dogs agree this is a good plan, as humans can do many things dogs cannot do. But it's also a dangerous plan because humans can make dogs do things like live in a house and wear jackets in winter and hats in the rain and other things no dog wants to do except maybe a silly dog like a Poodle.

Margaret runs off to the farmhouse while the other dogs hide behind some trees to wait. While they wait, the dogs say nice things to Fathead the Newfoundland when he complains about being stuck in the hole. After a few minutes, Margaret comes back with a human girl. The girl says something none of the dogs understand, then puts her hands to her mouth and laughs. After she finishes laughing, the girl goes to the other side of the barn where the dogs can't see her. A few minutes more pass, and the dogs see Fathead get pulled into the barn. Then Margaret appears and tells all the dogs to follow her.

Inside the barn, Fathead is lying on his side, looking lovingly at the girl while she strokes him. When the girl sees the other dogs come into the barn, she puts her hands to her mouth and laughs again. Then she jumps up, disappears, and comes back with a giant bag of dry dog food. She opens the bag, pours it into lots of dog bowls, and invites the dogs to eat.

"Friends are wonderful," says the Pug between bites of food.

"How are they wonderful?" asks the Dachshund, her mouth full of food.

"You are Fathead's friend, and you made him leader, even though he is too dumb to be our leader," begins Margaret. "Helmut is my friend, and he saved me when you said I was a bad dog. The girl is my friend, and she saved Fathead from being stuck under the barn."

"Now the girl is a friend to us all," adds Helmut, who can follow Margaret's idea even while he's eating.

"Fathead is wonderful," adds the Dachshund. "Because of Fathead, we all got this tasty food."

"Friends are wonderful," says Fathead the Newfoundland. "Even when they're dumb."

Here is the talk Tom and I had after I told him this story. "You say Fathead is dumb," Tom says. "What makes Fathead dumb?"

"Fathead is dumb because he does not know how to get what he wants," I answer.

"I don't know how to get what I want. Does that make me dumb?" Tom asks.

"Of course," I say. "But dumb in a different way. You don't know what you want."

Tom agrees.

"Why are the Dachshund and Fathead friends?" Tom asks. "They seem so different."

"You asked a why question. Why questions never answer anything. I will answer it as I answer any why question: make up any reason you want why they are friends. No one knows for sure. How they are friends is that they make each other happy and believe everything the other one says."

"How does believing everything I tell you make us friends?" Tom asks.

"Believing everything comes after we are friends," I say. "I know you are wrong about many things, but I still believe you when you tell me something. I learned to believe you when we became friends. I know you believe something when you say it to me, even when you are wrong."

"How can you believe something when you know it's wrong?"

"I believe that you believe it. What you say is true to you. It does not have to be true for me to believe it is true for you," I say.

"What if I tricked you?" Tom asks.

"Then we would not be friends anymore," I say.

CHAPTER SEVEN

ON THE CUSTOM OF PUTTING DOGS IN CLOTHES

"If I'm not enough for you without a hat, I'll never be enough with a hat, no matter how cute you think I look in a hat."

- Margaret the Pug

People do not understand their dogs. I will tell you how I know this. Dogs do not want to wear clothes. Tom and his mate have a sweater they put on me when they are cold. I do not need a sweater. No dog needs a sweater. Dogs have everything we need for every kind of weather.

"If you had a coat like mine, you'd wear the same outfit everyday, too."

- Lassie the TV dog

If it rains, the oil in our fur keeps us dry. A quick shake after we're inside makes us dry again. If it's cold, we breathe hard and warm ourselves up. We also have our fur which stands up and keeps our heat in. Our feet have pads and can handle rocks and cold. We have tails to cool ourselves and wrap our noses in. We need nothing to be comfortable. People need shoes for their feet. They need gloves for their hands and hats for their heads. Gloves, shoes, and hats are chew toys for us dogs. We don't need them to be comfortable when we're outside, only to help make us comfortable when we chew them inside.

People put clothes on their dogs because they want their dogs to be like them. Dogs are dogs. We are best when we are dogs and not people. This is how I know people don't understand their dogs. They want to make their dogs into people. Maybe there are some dogs who like clothes, but I don't know them, and they are not writing this book.

This is the only good thing about writing a book: I can speak for all dogs even though I am only one dog and do not know what all dogs think. I know what I think and what I think dogs should think. No dog should want to wear clothes. I will speak for all dogs and say all dogs do not like to wear clothes. If you do not believe me, you need to ask another dog. Any dog who wants to wear clothes should write its own book.

Dogs do not like to wear clothes because they make us look silly. Dogs are very patient and generous animals. People make us happy when they laugh and smile at us. People get excited when they see us in clothes, so we allow ourselves to be put in clothes, but not for very long because clothes are not a natural part of us. Dogs never beg for clothes as we do for food and affection. People should laugh and become excited when we do dog things like sniff out the biscuit that fell on the floor. But no. People become excited when they think we are acting like people by wearing clothes. This shows how people only see themselves. They look for human things in things that are not human. If humans did not wear clothes, they would see themselves more clearly. They do not see the animal in them which makes them like other animals.

I will tell you a story to show you how people want their animals to be like people, and that is why they put their animals in clothes instead of doing what they should, which is to take their clothes off so they can see themselves as they really are.

A Lonely Bear and a Lonely Man

A lonely man lives in the woods. He wants to find a dog to live with, but there are no dogs near him, and he does not want to go to town to find a dog because he is lazy. One day when the man is walking in the woods, he comes across a bear sitting by a stream. The bear looks sad, so the man asks, "Why are you sad?"

"I am lonely," says the bear. "I have no bears to live with. I would live with a dog if I could find one, but when I come near a dog, it runs away."

"I am lonely too," says the man. "We can live together and keep each other company since we can't find a dog to live with."

The bear agrees this is a good idea. The bear and the man walk back toward the man's house. They do not speak much while they are walking because a bear and a man do not have much to say to one another.

"I wish I had a dog to walk with instead of this bear," thinks the man. "But having a bear is better than having no one when you're a lonely man."

"I wish I had a dog to walk with," thinks the bear. "Dogs are more interesting than lonely men. Perhaps I will eat the man when we get back to his house. Then I will be refreshed, and I can look for dogs to walk with."

After some time, the bear and the man arrive at the man's house. "I am getting cold," the man says to the bear. "Come inside my house and put on one of my robes so I won't be cold." People are always telling someone to do something like 'put a robe on' not because they think it will help the other person, but because they think when the other person puts a robe on, they will feel better themselves. That's why people put dogs in hats or ask bears to put on a robe.

The bear is not cold because his coarse and smelly coat keeps him warm. It's not a smooth and soft coat like a Pug's coat, but it is all the coat the bear has and is good enough for living in the woods. The bear likes the man, so he follows the man inside his house and puts on one of his robes. The man smiles when the bear puts on his robe. "I feel much warmer now that you have a robe on," says the man. The bear likes that the man is happy, so he decides not to eat the man yet. He does not like the man's robe, though. It's too small and would pinch him in his armpits if he had arms instead of legs.

"What should we do now?" asks the bear. The bear and the man are not natural friends, so they don't know what to do together. The man thought the robe would make the bear more like a friend, but it just made the bear more uncomfortable.

"I will give you shoes to go with your robe, and a hat to keep your hair in while you cook me dinner." Now the bear decides he does not like the man so much, but he's still not quite ready to eat him. After all, the shoes might feel good on his feet, and the hat might make him look taller, so he lets the man dress him up. Once the bear gets into the man's shoes and puts on his hat, he looks in a mirror the man holds for him. He does look taller which makes him happy because being tall is very important to bears.

"Now you make us soup, and I will lie down here on the floor and rest," says the man to the bear. The man can see that the bear has never made soup before, so he turns the stove on, puts a pan full of water on the stove, and pulls food out of his cabinets and on the counter for the bear.

"Put what you like in the soup while I take a nap," says the man. "Wake me when the soup is ready." Then the man lays on the floor and goes to sleep.

The bear looks at the food the man has laid out for him. There are carrots, potatoes, chuck roast, berries, grain, and insects. The bear eats a carrot and thinks. The man looks nice while he is sleeping, and it's good to have company and something to eat. The bear decides to eat all the food and watch the man sleep. After the bear finishes the chuck roast and berries, the man wakes up.

"Where is our soup?" asks the man.

"I ate it," says the bear.

The man gets up from the floor and goes to the stove. All the water has boiled out of the pot, and there is no soup. His chuck roast, carrots, potatoes, berries, and grain are all gone. Only the insects are left.

"You never made any soup," the man tells the bear. "I can tell because there is a burn mark on the bottom of my pot where you left it on the stove with no water."

The bear tries to shrug his shoulders to show he agrees, but the robe is too tight. "Perhaps we should not live together," says the bear.

"Perhaps not," agrees the man. "You will not make a good roommate, even if you do look good in my robe."

What does this story mean? Putting a robe on a bear will not get you soup. It also means we dress each other up to be what we want. Putting a robe on a bear does not make the bear a good roommate. A bear is a bear, and a dog is a dog. Neither will ever be comfortable in a robe or a raincoat. Robes and raincoats are for making humans comfortable, not for bears or dogs.

CHAPTER EIGHT

THE EMPEROR'S OLD PUG

"I have no idea what anything means, which means I get to decide what everything means for myself."
- Margaret the Pug

In the morning, after breakfast, I go to the front door to look at my reflection. I also look for dogs outside and bark at them. I bark, and the dogs go away. Barking makes the mailman go away, too. The story "Barking Makes Things Go Away" explains what happens when I bark. The story "Mailmen Don't Like Pugs" works just like "Barking Makes the Mailman Go Away," but I know "Mailmen Don't Like Pugs" is a silly story because everyone likes Pugs.

"Everyone likes Pugs. Anyone who doesn't like Pugs needs to go away."

- George Washington's Weimaraner

I want to show you how we take the same things and make different stories from them. One story is a human story, and the other story is a Pug's story. Both stories are made from the same things.

Here is the human story: There is a very foolish and proud emperor who loves clothes. One day two bad people come to his town and say they are tailors who make clothes so fine and beautiful that only fine people can see them. Because the emperor is foolish and proud and does not want to admit he can't see the clothes that only fine people can see, he says he sees the clothes even though he can't because the clothes are just pretend. The tailors make a lot of money, and the emperor ends up walking around in his underwear. This story makes my head hurt.

Now for the dog's story. This story has lots of details because dogs pay close attention to everything, unlike people who are always moving from one thing to another and won't say they can't see something because it's embarrassing.

The Pug, the Emperor, and the Men with Nothing in Their Arms

There is a human emperor who has a Pug—a Pug like myself—the finest and smartest breed of dog. She is such a fine Pug we will call her Margaret. Margaret goes everywhere with her emperor, to shops and restaurants and markets. Where the emperor lives, Pugs can go everywhere. It is not like here, where humans have to leave their Pugs behind. One afternoon, Margaret goes with the emperor to the place where the emperor gets his clothes. These are new clothes, not fine-smelling old clothes, so they are not interesting. On this afternoon the clothing-making-humans are very excited and talk to the emperor about something pretend the two men are holding in their arms. The emperor is nodding his head and smiling while the clothing-making-humans talk, but there is nothing to nod about because the clothing-making-humans have nothing in their arms. Margaret becomes confused, which does not happen often because Pugs are very smart and have good priorities. Margaret thinks, "What is the emperor smiling at? The sunshine on the rug is very nice, but the emperor has never smiled at that before. There's a lovely smell of old meat and aged wine here, but the emperor likes fresh meat and new wine.

What is he smiling at?" Margaret looks all over the shop but can't find anything to smile about. After some time, the emperor waves at the clothing-making-humans and leaves the shop with Margaret still confused.

More time goes by, and Margaret and the emperor return to the shop. The clothing-making-humans are there, smiling and nodding their heads and waving their arms, and soon the emperor begins to nod his head, too. Then the emperor goes behind a curtain and comes back out in his underwear. The clothing-making-humans clap and wave their arms and look very happy. Seeing him in his underwear is nothing new, but Margaret becomes happy since everyone is so happy to see the emperor in his underwear. After a few minutes of strutting about the shop in his underwear, the emperor goes behind the curtain again, puts his clothes back on, and goes home with Margaret.

More time goes by and one day the clothing-making-humans come to the house where the emperor and Margaret live. The clothing-making-humans look very proud. They have a big box with them. The four of them—the emperor, Margaret, and the two clothing-making-humans—run up to the emperor and Margaret's bedroom. Some humans who carry things bring the big box into the bedroom, and the emperor shushes them away. The four are alone together—Margaret, the emperor, and the humans who make clothes. They look at each other, happy to be alone together. What will happen next?

The clothing-making-humans open the box, and nothing is inside. Margaret is disappointed. Something to eat should be in the box instead of nothing. Margaret looks at her emperor. The emperor is not disappointed. The emperor is smiling with his eyebrows up. He's scared! Margaret knows the emperor is scared because she smells it, even though he's trying to make his excited face. Why would the emperor be scared of nothing? Margaret is very confused now. The humans who make clothes are not scared. They are excited. Margaret can smell that, too. What are the humans who make clothes excited about? The box is empty. Why did they bring an empty box all the way to Margaret's house? This is a question with no good answer.

One of the humans who makes clothes acts like he's pulling something out of the box and motions with his head for the emperor to come close to him. Margaret is suspicious now.

She growls to tell her emperor not to go to the human who makes clothes, and the emperor snaps at her. This is a very silly emperor. The emperor takes another step toward the clothing-making-human with nothing in his arms, and Margaret barks again. The emperor scolds Margaret because he is a bad emperor, but his Pug loves him anyway. Again the emperor reaches out to touch the thing that's not there, and Margaret barks and barks and barks. The emperor gets the clothing-making-humans to slam the big box shut, which is good, but he also calls one of his humans who moves things to come and pick up Margaret and carry her out of the room. This makes Margaret sad because Pugs don't like being away from their emperors even when their emperors are acting strangely.

Why would the emperor put her out of the room? Then Margaret thinks the emperor must like the clothing-making-humans better than her. It makes no sense. He has known the clothing-making-humans for a very short time while he has known Margaret for years. This is terrible because Margaret does not like the clothing-making-humans at all. They are doing something to the emperor; they are telling the emperor a story that Margaret does not understand. After a long time, the door to the bedroom opens, and the humans who make clothes come out, each carrying a large, heavy sack that smells like coins. Margaret growls at them as they go down the stairs, but her mood brightens when the emperor lets her back into his room. The emperor is in his underwear again. The emperor play-scolds Margaret, and she knows it's play, so she lays down on the rug on her back and smiles up at the emperor, who smiles back at her and scratches her belly. Everything is good again.

More time goes by. The emperor has been planning something with all his helpers. Today is the day of the thing they have been planning. The emperor is going somewhere. After breakfast, the emperor sends Margaret out of the bedroom and downstairs with all the helpers. They are talking and waiting for something exciting like grilled chicken or peanut butter. One of the humans who carries things has Margaret in his arms. All the helpers are facing the stairs. They are waiting for the emperor. A moment goes by, and the emperor appears at the top of the stairs. He has his crown on, and he's holding his scepter, and he's in his underwear again. Everyone applauds. Margaret is confused. Are they applauding because the emperor is letting them see him in his underwear? Margaret sees the applause is making the emperor happy. She thinks, "Why is the emperor showing everyone his underwear?" Margaret thinks some more. When does the emperor usually walk around in his underwear? Before he goes to bed! Margaret sleeps with the emperor, so she knows he wears his underwear beforehegoestobedandwhenhewakesup.It'stoolatetowakeup, so the emperor must be getting ready to go to bed. The emperor is going to go to bed with all his helpers, and that's why he's in his underwear! Now things make sense, and Margaret smiles.

The emperor is all the way down the stairs now, and he walks toward Margaret. He reaches out his arms, and one of the humans who hold things gives the Pug to the emperor, and the emperor hands his scepter to the human so the human will have something else to hold. Together the emperor and Margaret go outside and get in their carriage. They are going some place. When will they go to bed with everyone? That must be coming sometime soon but not now.

The emperor and Margaret snuggle up together in the carriage. The emperor wears his crown and his underwear while Margaret sits on a blanket. They are happy together as the horses pull the carriage through the gates. Outside the gates, people are standing along the streets. Lines of people stretch along both sides of the road. The town humans are waving and cheering for Margaret and her emperor. What a beautiful day! Pugs and emperors are worth cheering for even when they're in their underwear, but Margaret and the emperor have ridden in the carriage before, even on days as beautiful as this day, and the town humans have not gathered

to cheer for them. What's different today? The emperor is in his underwear. Are all the town humans going to bed with the Pug, the emperor, and his helpers? How will they fit?

While the Pug is wondering where all the town humans and helper humans will fit in the bedroom, a commotion happens. A little human is pointing at the emperor. He's saying something that makes all the humans afraid. The emperor is afraid, too. Then the people begin to laugh. They're pointing and laughing at the emperor. Like all good Pugs, Margaret likes laughter, but the emperor does not like this laughter. The emperor gets angry. Why is the emperor angry? Margaret is not angry; laughter is fun. The emperor orders something to the human who drives the carriage and they continue their ride. All along the ride, the town humans point at the emperor and shout and laugh. The emperor feels worse and worse but holds his head up. He's pretending not to hear the laughter or be bothered by it. Margaret knows he's pretending because no one knows a emperor like his Pug. After a long ride that Margaret enjoys very much, Margaret and the emperor come home. No one sleeps with them. Not even Margaret sleeps with the emperor because the emperor is angry with her for no reason, which is very unfair, but that's how emperors are, and that's why Pugs are so strong because they love their emperors anyway. No one saw the tailors again, and the emperor stopped wearing his underwear in public. After a brief period of having fewer dishes to lick as the emperor did not have as much company as usual, life for the Pug went on as before.

What does this story mean? To the Pug, it means carriage rides are fun, especially when lots of people are looking at you, and you are looking back at them. What does it mean to the emperor? Who knows. It should mean, "Always trust your Pug."

Final Thoughts

This book is the first in a series on the philosophy of Margaret the Pug. Like all dogs, Margaret has a lot to say. Look for volume 2 of *A Dog's Book of Wisdom* where you got this copy or at dogsbookofwisdom.com.

If you want to learn more about Margaret visit her at margaretthepug.com.

If you want to spread the word about dog wisdom by carrying *A Dog's Book of Wisdom* in your own establishment, contact us at hello@dogsbookofwisdom.com.

Margaret and Tom want to thank everyone who helped bring her ideas to a wider audience, particularly Dani Long, Logan Pyron, Emma Oxford, Mark Cowden, Jennifer Piceno, and most especially Jerry Park without whose advice and help this book would never have been born.

If you want to help Pugs who don't have homes, consider making a donation to the Pug rescue organization in your area. If you want to help Poodles, we think you should reevaluate your priorities.